Chakra Recipe Guide

Chakra Recipe Guide

Quick and Easy Recipes for Chakras 2 to 6

Artimia Arian

iUniverse, Inc.

New York Lincoln Shanghai

Chakra Recipe Guide
Quick and Easy Recipes for Chakras 2 to 6

iUniverse, Inc.

For information address:
iUniverse
2021 Pine Lake Road, Suite 100
Lincoln, NE 68512
www.iuniverse.com

ISBN: 0-595-28425-6

Printed in the United States of America

Dedication

*To **LIFE** and all those who are ready to shun dis-ease and death and embrace the knowledge which leads to Life. Learn to love yourself by becoming master of your mind, rather than a slave to your desires. Give yourself the best so as to be able to give of your best to others.*

Death promotes disease and decay. Life generates Life. Become only Life so as to become a Life-Giver for humanity. Tashirat is the highest path of Truth, Love and Life. To attain the highest, one has to give one's utmost. Give your all and you'll receive All.

Learn the psychology of mind control. Discipline yourself kindly and wisely as you would discipline a child. Learn when to give in a little to your desires, being flexible, and when to be firm and rigid. Through the art of self-discipline, tame your desires and eventually dominate them, transcending the physical and lower emotional realms to heights usually unattainable by the human. One's discipline should neither be too rigid nor too lax. Aim at moderation in all aspects of life.

Enjoy your evolutionary journey as your consciousness expands, using food as a potent tool of creation rather than destruction. Learn to value and regenerate this inconceivably incredible human body machine; cherish it and recognize it for what it is—a temple for the Spirit. One's spiritual journey in Chakra 4 has not fully commenced, until one has begun one's dietary discipline, which is Chakra 3's life lesson.

*Happy eating! Happy living! To **LIFE**.*

Live your beliefs and you can turn the world around.

Henry Thoreau

Contents

Vibration

Everything in the Universe vibrates at a certain frequency. The higher we raise our vibration, the higher our energy level, the more orderly, the happier and the more harmonious we become.

Everything possesses its own unique vibratory frequency—each mineral, plant, animal, human, food, color, music, room, home, country, etc. People's tastes vary according to their vibration. A higher vibration individual lives a clean, neat, orderly and harmonious life. S/he will select food, colors, music, friends, work etc. of a high vibration. A lower vibration individual lives in disharmony due to a chaotic mind which is unable to achieve order. A whirl-wind of chaos and noise is created by a lower vibration person's mind, negatively affecting his / her own life and the lives of others around him / her.

Discipline and love are required to raise one's vibration. The three discipline chakras are Chakras 1, 3 and 5. In Chakra 1, one disciplines oneself to fulfil one's job requirements. Punctuality, reliability, responsibility, stability are required. (Note these qualities are fundamental to all the chakra lessons which follow). In Chakra 3, one implements a healthy dietary discipline, avoiding foods which are harmful, consuming foods and food combinations which are nutritious and easy to digest. In Chakra 5, one works the mental body with study and one learns tongue control.

Most people on Earth do not follow any dietary discipline, their taste buds dictate their dietary habits. What is ingested is not generally related to one's state of health. At Tashirat Headquarters in Tepoztlan we have proved with our own bodies and with the bodies of so many students, that healthy food is one of the most important factors contributing to a high level of health.

Tashirat is a path of Truth, Love and Life. The tools we use to raise our vibration as we attempt to walk this highest path are: Hatha Yoga, Pranayama, Meditation, Nutrition, Selfless Service in the community, Study, and Following a Daily program which includes all of the above.

This Food Chakra Chart was received in a meditation. It is extremely valuable knowledge and a powerful tool once one learns how to utilize it.

A food's vibration is the sum total of its nutritive quality and its digestibility. The higher the vibration, the more nutritious and the easier it is to digest. The lower the vibration, the less nutritious and the more difficult it is to digest. High vibratory foods produce clarity of thought and perception, calmness; low vibratory foods produce denseness, insensitivity, limited vision, an agitated or dull mind. High vibration foods (Chakras 4, 5 and 6) nourish and minerally balance the physical vehicle. Low vibration foods (Chakras 1, 2 and 3 if eaten in excess) clog the physical body, leading to mineral imbalances, toxicity, and eventually dis-ease.

Our lives must be coherent in order for us to achieve that balance, fulfilment, peace, happiness and harmony that we all naturally seek as we evolve toward the Light. For our lives to be coherent, our work, food, environment, people in our lives etc. should be of a similar vibration. A person cannot attain physical health or emotional stability and happiness, unless s/he is doing the correct life work according to his / her vibration, eating the correct vibration of food, and living in the right environment for his / her vibration. These three factors are basic to health which is balance, a unique balance achieved according to the individual's evolution.

The food chakra vibration that an individual requires to achieve a state of health, will vary from person to person. It will depend upon the person's present condition, present dietary habits, and his / her evolution (i.e. what chakra the person attained in a past life). It is imperative that we eat, work and live according to our evolution. A person who reached Chakra 5 in a past life, will become seriously ill if s/he eats flesh foods (Chakra 1) or dairy products (Chakra 2) indefinitely in this lifetime. However a person who never got to Chakra 2 in a past life, would do well with dairy products in this life for some time, until ready to move up to carbohydrates in Chakra 3.

Eating above or below one's chakra vibration can create a negative emotional state such as general unhappiness, frustration or irritability. Eating below one's chakra vibration over an extended period of time will result in toxic accumulations in the body. Eating above one's chakra vibration for extended periods will create emotional dissatisfaction and imbalance or if the body is extremely toxic, a dangerously fast elimination which the body is unable to cope with.

Regardless of what chakra one attained in a past life, it is not advisable to skip food chakras in this lifetime. It is best for the physical and emotional bodies to live a comfortable but steady transition to higher chakras in this lifetime. The only time this would not apply, would be in the case of chronic illness.

A person who attained a high chakra in a past life, will be more affected by low vibration foods than someone who never reached a high vibration. For example, an individual who reached Chakra 5 or 6 in a past life, will not do well on dairy products or cooked carbohydrates for a whole lifetime. Usually problems set in in the forties. To attain health, which is balance, we must return to the chakra we attained in a past lifetime as soon as possible—meaning our food, work and whole lifestyle are in harmony with the chakra vibration.

Natural food is our medicine and our principal medicine should be our food. Minerally balanced food creates minerally balanced bodies. Minerally balanced food requires minerally balanced soil. We all need to begin our own cultivation so as to consume pesticide-free, balanced fruit and vegetables.

Prevention is so much better and easier than trying to cure chronic or degenerative dis-ease imbalances. Slow but steady purification and strengthening of the physical body, through a consistent gradual dietary transition from lower vibration foods to higher vibration foods, is the ideal. It is so much healthier physically and emotionally. Stringent long fasts or excessively rigid dietary regimes are all too frequently counter-productive, as they too often conclude in bouts of destructive binging. Moderation, balance is our goal, as we gradually but happily progress along our paths.

Food Chakra Chart

Chakra 1   Flesh foods, Garlic.

Chakra 2   Eggs, Dairy Products, Legumes, Mushrooms, Eggplant, Onion, Chile, Radish.

Chakra 3   Complex Carbohydrates (grains, pastas, bread, tortillas, potatoes and other tubercles, corn on the cob), Seaweed, Avocado, Tofu.

Chakra 4   Lightly steamed or sautéed Vegetables, Lightly cooked Vegetable Soups, Dehydrated foods, Nuts and Seeds, Nopales.

Chakra 5   Raw Vegetable Salads and Soups, Vegetable Drinks, Sprouts, Green leaves, Weeds.

Chakra 6   Fruit, Fruit Drinks, Green Chlorophyll Drinks, Honey.

Chakra 7   Prana.

Useful Dietary Knowledge

The Food Chakra Chart is information that was received in a meditation. However, this information has become knowledge, as it was lived and confirmed. All information in this book is confirmed knowledge which has been tested on and lived by many people.

In my experience with people of all vibrations (even the very lowest), an over-consumption of flesh food results in painful chronic conditions such as arthritis, rheumatism, gout, constipation (which is the source of all ills), migraines, hives or any other form of eczema, sciatica, Bright's Disease (kidney inflammation) or any other kidney trouble, insomnia, gastritis, bronchitis, and all the other "—itis" inflammatory conditions which are associated with high levels of uric acid.

The human is not constructed to consume flesh foods. Destroying a life, stunting an animal's natural evolution, is a violation of the Universal Laws, laws which control the Universe energetically. Creative acts of love and life, increase our force. Destructive acts of aggression and violence, diminish our force. Continual acts of destruction lead to degeneration and eventual death.

Flesh foods can perhaps sustain life for some time but the consumption of flesh foods inevitably leads to premature death at its best and prolonged suffering before death for the invalid and for all those involved in his / her life, at its worst. Dead flesh foods cannot construct, regenerate and create life. Life creates Life.

Chakra 1, flesh food recipes are not even included in this book, as flesh food is deemed unfit for human consumption. However if you are still eating flesh food daily, eliminate red meat immediately, and slowly reduce your fish and chicken intake, if you feel you are presently unable to eliminate it completely from your diet.

Sugar is a drug, unrecognized as such, freely consumed by most and given to children liberally from an early age. It creates havoc in the body. Amongst its numerable disastrous side effects, it destroys the immune system, lowering the body's defences; creates a total mineral imbalance in the body, negatively affecting the entire bodily metabolism; destroys the glandular system and the nervous system, once again impeding physical and emotional balance and health; destroys the teeth and bones-calcium is leeched from the teeth and bones due to the mineral imbalance. All sugar (white and brown) and any food item containing it (read labels) and all refined products (white rice, white spaghetti, white bread, etc.) must be removed from the diet entirely if one wants to be healthy.

Dairy products result in high levels of blood acidity and mucosity. Buttermilk, yoghurt, cottage cheese, panela and riqueson are the best options while transitioning.

Cooked complex carbohydrates such as bread, potatoes, tortillas, pastas and grains, even the best quality whole wheat pastas or whole grain rice, also create blood acidity and high levels of mucosity, if consumed in excess over a number of years. Over time they result in a mucus-congested digestive tract and organism in general, impeding the assimilation of nutrients. The organic minerals in carbohydrates become inorganic once cooked and the body is not able to assimilate them. They therefore accumulate in the body collecting in organs such as the gall bladder, creating gall bladder stones. The liver is thus affected, as a clean healthy gall bladder is essential to the proper functioning of the liver. The digestion is affected. The kidneys are affected too, having to eliminate granular secretions, gravel. Such accumulations ultimately lead to chronic problems, if the root of the problem is not eradicated. All these cooked complex carbohydrates are full of inorganic calcium and other inorganic matter. Even the healthiest, sprouted, dehydrated grain bread, produces mucosity. If the body is not already acidic, they can be eaten in small quantities with an abundance of lightly steamed and fresh vegetables. Complex carbohydrates (even the sprouted grains) are, never-the-less, not an ideal food for the human.

The healthiest foods are Chakra 4, 5 and 6 foods as they nourish the body without burdening it with toxic accumulations. Chakra 4—lightly steamed or dehydrated vegetables or vegetable soups, soaked nuts and sprouted seeds (not in excess as they can also create acidity). Chakra 5—raw vegetables and vegetable juices or soups, sprouts. Chakra 6—green leaves and chlorophyll drinks, fruit.

If eating a Chakra 2 diet, eat approximately 60% raw and 40% Chakra 2 and above. If eating a Chakra 3 diet, eat about 70% raw and 30% cooked (Chakra 3 and above). For a Chakra 4 diet, eat 80% raw and 20% Chakra 4 diet. Chakras 5 and 6 are totally raw.

All oil must be cold-pressed and unrefined. In Mexico the extra virgen olive oil is good.

In Chakras 1 to 4 one can substitute iodized salt with sea salt, soy sauce or tamari or any vegetable substitute. However, once one is on Chakra 5, all raw, one should rather use Bragg or seaweeds that are not too salty e.g. hijiki, nori, kelp. In Chakra 6 even Bragg is eliminated. Some unsalty seaweed can be utilized in small quantities. Cayenne or fresh chiles can be employed in moderation, to overcome the salt craving, provided they do not irritate the digestive tract e.g. causing diarrea.

Ensure a wide variety of food items in your diet, thus ensuring an ample supply of all the necessary vitamins and minerals. Create attractive dishes. Visual appeal is of the utmost importance. Experiment with different forms of cutting and arranging the dishes. Use attractive plates. Plates can be decorated with fruits, vegetables, flowers and leaves.

Useful Kitchen Tips

1. To Disinfect

i) For every liter of water, add the juice of 2 lemons and 1 tbs. of sea salt. Wash the vegetables well with tap water and soak them in this lemon-salt water for 15 minutes (no more than 15 mins. or they absorb the salt).

ii) Place a small bundle of wheatgrass tied with string or a rubber band, in your water. Wash the vegetables thoroughly and soak them in the wheatgrass water for 10–15 mins. The wheatgrass can be used afterwards.

iii) There are various commercial but natural disinfecting products that can be purchased. Nutribiotic is a good one.

2. To Sprout

i) Soak the seeds in a bowl of water overnight. (Different seeds in different bowls).

ii) Remove the water in the morning, using a large strainer.

iii) Place the seeds in a large plate or tray and cover them with a humid cloth.

iv) Wet the seeds and cloth twice a day, morning and night, never keeping them too wet, but never allowing them to dry.

v) Within 3–7 days (depending on the seeds) your sprouts will be ready. They are ready to eat once the first two green leaves appear.

vi) They are best eaten fresh, but can be refrigerated in tuppers or plastic bags.

3. Healthy Substitutes

• Iodized salt must be eliminated. Iodized salt substitutes for Chakras 2, 3 and 4 are: sea salt, tamari, soy sauce miso. As they all contain a lot of salt, they should be used sparingly. Once on raw food i.e. Chakras 5 and 6, sea salt, tamari, soy sauce and miso are best substituted with any of the seaweeds such as kelp or dulse and Bragg (liquid aminos made in the USA). The seaweeds are superior to the Bragg. The closer one approaches Chakra 6, the more Bragg will have to be avoided, and unsalty seaweeds such as nori or hijiki can be used in small quantities. Obviously Bragg and especially **seaweeds** are the best iodized salt substitutes for all the chakras. The seaweeds are valuable mineral sources. Kelp contains much iodine. Train yourself to gradually cut down on excess salty and sweet food (even if healthy), as the taste buds become more refined.

- **Honey** is an excellent sugar substitute, but used in moderation. Limit the honey intake to 1 tbs. per day. Natural sugars found in fruits are best.

- **Cayenne or Fresh or Dried Chiles** are good black or white pepper substitutes. Chile is a stimulant which can aid circulation, digestion and elimination if eaten sparingly and wisely. In large quantities it is an irritant. The closer one approaches Chakra 6, the more it will have to be omitted.

- **Carob** is a substitute for chocolate, and has no toxic side effects.

- **Cold-pressed unrefined oils such as olive oil, sunflower, sesame or coconut oil** are good substitutes for all oils and butter. When olive oil has been cold pressed, it still contains the green chlorophyll. Although healthy, the cold pressed oils are highly concentrated and should be used sparingly. The closer one approaches Chakra 6, the more they will create nausea and will naturally be eliminated eventually. Oils are found naturally within nature's foods such as avocadoes, nuts, seeds and olives.

4. Condiments

Especially in the beginning of your healthier diet, condiments are a necessary addition, used in moderation, to enhance flavoring. Good condiments are seaweed such as kelp or dulse, lemon juice, herbs and natural, home-made vegetable and herb-weed dried powders.

- **Salt**—If you are accustomed to a high salt intake, in the transition it would be best to use it in the form of tamari or miso, both of which are fermented soy products, containing about 20% sea salt and many enzymes. Preferable salt substitutes are one of the vegetable salt substitutes, Bragg, kelp powder or other seaweed. (If in Mexico you cannot find kelp powder, buy kelp capsules in a health food store, open them and sprinkle the contents on the food).

- **Home-made Vegetable / Herb Salt Substitutes**—Herbs or greens can be bunched and hung for drying in a warm, ventilated room or shelter, or spread on drying racks. (Herbs should not be dried in the sun). Alternatively use a dehydrator. When dry, put them in the blender, grind them to flakes or powders and use them in salad dressings, soups, or sprinkled on salads or breads. Good vegetable flavorings include: garlic, onion, beets, radish, celery stalks and leaves, carrots, zucchini, tomato, ginger, or anything else of your choice. Useful herbs or greens for flavoring are: parsley, spinach, carrot tops, radish tops, beet tops, arugula, watercress, basil, oragano, thyme, mint, onion and garlic leaves. It is good to bottle and label the dried vegetable flakes and powders separately, and then also keep a few different combinations handy.

- **Spices and Aromatic Seeds**—These can be purchased in most health food stores. Spices such as curry, cinnamon, clove, nutmeg, vanilla are always good to keep. In addition aromatic seeds like anise, caraway, cumin, dill and mustard are useful. Herbs and spices should be used in small amounts. Vegetables and vegetable tops can be used freely. No seasoning should ever be used in excess, they should enhance and complement, not replace the flavors of any of the foods. Excessive seasoning can cause digestive and kidney problems with time.

Food Combining Guidelines

1. Do not mix proteins with carbohydrates.

Proteins: Red meat, chicken, fish; Dairy products—milk, butter, yoghurt, cream; Eggs; Legumes—beans, lentils, soy products such as tofu; Nuts and seeds.

Carbohydrates: Grains—rice, oatmeal, wheat, millet, etc; Pasta; Bread and tortilla; Avocado; Tubercles—potatoes, sweet potatoes, cooked carrot and beet.

2. Proteins and Carbohydrates combine well with a raw vegetable salad and with pure corn tortillas. Eat one carbohydrate or one protein with steamed vegetables, a raw salad and tortillas.

3. Fruit—Always eat fruit alone. Citric or acid fruit does not combine very well with sweet fruit.

Citric Fruit: Oranges, mandarins, pineapple, grapefruit, etc.

Sweet Fruit: Banana, dried fruit, mamey, etc.

****

How much time must one wait after eating a meal, before eating again ?

i)   *Most fruit digests in 20-30 mins. Dried fruit, banana and all melons take longer–40-60 mins.*

ii)   *After a raw vegetable meal, wait 2 hours.*

iii)   *After a well combined raw and cooked food meal, wait 3 hours.*

iv)   *After a poorly combined meal, wait at least 8 hours. (Help with an enema).*

Simple Salad Dressings

Throughout the book, practical, quick and easy recipe guidelines are offered, providing you with a simplified food preparation manual, enabling you to eat healthy, tasty food, but not spend hours shopping or in the kitchen. This manual is designed to assist you in organizing your kitchen for yourself and your family. Surprisingly by ordering the kitchen, one's whole life becomes more organized, and of a higher quality.

These are not always exact recipes with exact measurements. Ingredients are given and a clear guideline as to the method, but you are encouraged to get the general gist of what each chakra entails foodwise, and from the base provided, create delicious healthy food with what you have available in the kitchen, and according to your unique taste and style.

Good salad dressings can be created by selecting one dressing base and combining it with any of the following seasonings. Add the salt substitute of your choice (refer to Useful Kitchen Tips chapter, Healthy Substitutes). Add olive oil (or other) and / or water as desired. All salad dressings are concocted in a few minutes by simply blending all the ingredients in the blender.

Dressings and sauces are the key to delicious food preparation. The food can be simple, but served with a great dressing or sauce e.g. steamed vegetables, raw vegetables sliced or combined in salads, rice or pasta, served with any of the following dressings (watch the food combinations).

Dressing Base

1. Avocado
2. Vegetables
3. Nuts and Seeds
4. Chilis
5. Oil (cold-pressed, unrefined) and Lemon Juice or Vinegar
6. Sun-Dried Tomatoes

Seasonings

1. Herbs (cilantro, basil, parsley, mint, any other)
2. Chili
3. Onion, Garlic
4. Vegetables (red pepper, fresh or dried tomatoes)
5. Ginger
6. Apple cider vinegar
7. Lemon juice or orange juice
8. Aromatic seeds (anise, caraway, cumin, dill, mustard)
9. Spices (curry, clove, nutmeg, cinnamon)

1. Avocado Dressing Examples

- Blend: Avocado, basil, lemon (optional), garlic, Bragg (or other salt substitute), oil or water.
- For 1 liter of dressing blend: 4 Avocados, cilantro, 1 clove of garlic, onion, salt substitute, juice of 2 lemons, fresh chili (optional), water.
- Blend: Avocadoes, vegetables of choice, salt substitute, juice of lemons or vinegar, herbs of choice e.g. tomatoes, onion, cilantro, avocadoes, lemon, Bragg, green chili (optional).
- Italian Dressing. Blend: olive oil, vinegar, Italian herbs, mustard, Bragg.

2. Vegetable Dressing Examples

- For 1 lt. Blend: olive oil, water, Bragg, ¼ large onion, 1 tomato, 1 large carrot, 1 small chili serrano, juice of 1 lemon, little apple cider vinegar.
- Blend: Cilantro, miso, olive oil, red pepper, carrot, garlic, tomato.
- Blend: 1 tsp dried basil, 1 carrot, ¼ jalapeno chili, ¼ red bell pepper, ½ orange juiced, 1 tsp. Bragg, 1 tsp. onion, 1 tsp. olive oil, ¾ cup water.

- Vegetable Carrot Dressing. Blend: 1 tsp. basil, 2 carrots, pinch of cayenne, ½ red pepper, juice of 1 orange, 1 tbs. olive oil, little onion, 1 tsp. Bragg, ¾ cup water.

- Blend vegetables of choice such as: tomatoes, celery, zucchini, carrots, cucumber, bell pepper, herbs of choice, oil, Bragg, water, lemon juice or apple cider vinegar, garlic, onion.

3. Nut and Seed Dressing Examples

- For thick creamy nut-seed mayonnaise dressings blend: soaked seeds and nuts, Bragg (miso or other substitute), oil & / water, herb (basil or other), garlic, red bell pepper & / sun-dried tomatoes, chili (if want it hot), mustard (optional), honey (optional), lemon juice or vinegar.

- Blend: sprouted sunflower & / sesame seeds, Bragg, water, lemon or vinegar, chili (optional), olive oil (optional), herbs of choice, honey (optional).

- Blend: 4 tbs. sprouted sunflower seeds, 1 chili chipotle in vinegar, ¼ red pepper, 1 tbs. Bragg, ½ cup water, 1 tbs. olive oil.

- Mayonnaise. Blend: ½ cup lemon juice, 2 tbs. honey, 2 tbs. tahini, ¼ cup olive oil (or less).

- Alternative Mayonnaise Dressings. Blend: 1 cup sprouted sunflower seeds (or soaked almonds or pecans), ¼ cup (or less) olive oil, juice of 1 lemon, 1 tbs. apple cider vinegar, 1 tsp. honey, 1 tsp. paprika, 1 tsp. mustard, 1 clove garlic, Bragg, water.

- Almond Dressing. Blend: soaked almonds (hazel nuts, walnuts or pecans), parsley, chives, garlic, celery, bell peppers (red, green, yellow), olive oil, Bragg, water.

- 1000 Island Dressing. Blend: ½ cup sprouted sunflower seeds, lemon juice or vinegar, olive oil, Bragg, 1 red bell pepper, 1 small onion, a little celery.

- Pine Nut Dressing. Blend: pine nuts, oil, basil, garlic (optional), red bell peppers, Bragg, mustard (optional), cayenne or fresh or dried chili (if want hot).

- Light Sesame Dressing. Blend: sesame seed or olive oil, sesame seeds sprouted or lightly toasted, Bragg or tamari, lemon, water.

- Blend: Soaked almond or sunflower seeds, orange juice, chili chipotle, red pepper, curry, Bragg, water.

15

- Sesame Ginger Dressing. Blend: 2tbs. tahini or 3 tbs. soaked sesame seeds, a small piece of ginger, ¼ clove of garlic, 1 tsp. honey, lemon (optional).
- To make 1 cup, blend: 2 tbs. soaked sunflower seeds, garlic, ½ tsp. miso, ½ tsp. Bragg, juice of 1 lemon, ¼ red bell pepper, 1 cup water.
- Mint Dressing. To make 1 cup, blend: 2 tbs. soaked sunflower seeds, 2 tbs. fresh mint, ¼ cucumber, 1 lemon, 1 tsp. Bragg, 1 cup water.

4. Chili Dressing Examples

Dried chilis (guajillo, ancho, pasilla) must be deveined, de-seeded and soaked 15–30 mins. until soft in warm or hot water before blending.

- Blend: chili serrano (or other fresh or dried chili), olive oil, Bragg, water, lemon juice, cilantro (or other herb).
- Chili Tahini Dressing. Blend: tahini, chili ancho, olive oil (optional), garlic (optional), bell pepper, Bragg or soy sauce, water.
- Chili Guajillo Sauce. Blend: 6 chili guajillos, juice of 1 orange, water, 1–2 tbs. vinegar, ¼ small onion, little miso, olive oil, little ginger, garlic and curry powder (optional, or alternatively use cumin and organo).
- Mexican Salsa Verde (Chili Green Tomato Sauce). Blend: lots of green tomatoes, 1–2 green chilis (serrano or jalapeño—jalapeño is milder), some onion, lots of cilantro, garlic (optional), Bragg or sea salt, water.
- Mexican Sauce. Blend: tomatoes, onion, cilantro, Bragg, fresh green chilis, lemon (optional). Dice: tomatoes, onion, cilantro. Mix everything together.
- Blend: Tomatoes, chili guajillo, garlic & onion (optional), Bragg (or other salt substitute).

5. Oil and Lemon Dressing Examples

- Herb Dressing. Blend: Water, Bragg, cilantro, cayenne or other fresh or dried chili, fresh or powdered ginger and onion, cumin, Italian herbs.
- Blend: Olive oil, lemon, ginger, honey, mustard, Bragg.

- Blend: 2 parts olive oil, 1 part vinegar (pure apple cider), garlic (optional), any seasonal herbs (parsley, oregano, basil, thyme, Italian herb mix, etc.), salt substitute.
- Mustard Vinagrette. Blend: ½ cup oil, 1 lemon, 1 tsp. Italian herbs, 1 tsp mustard, 1 tsp honey.
- Blend: 2 tbs. miso, 2 tbs. onion, 1 clove garlic, ½ cup lemon juice, ½ cup orange juice, ¼ cup olive oil, ¼ cup water.

6. Sun-Dried Tomato Dressing Examples

- Blend: fresh tomatoes, sun-dried tomatoes, basil, garlic, honey or 1 date, little olive oil, water.
- Blend: sun-dried tomatoes, juice of 1 or 2 lemons, miso or Bragg, pinch cumin seed, little olive oil, green chili, water.
- CATSUP # 1 Blend: sun-dried tomatoes, 2–3 dates, onion, garlic, 1–2 tsp basil, ½ red pepper, 1 tsp. olive oil.
- CATSUP # 2 Blend: soaked chili guallilos, honey or raisins, piece of garlic, piece of onion, pinch of grounded cumin, 1 clove grounded, quite a lot of water. Strain and eat as catsup with patties or with salads, steamed veggies, raw veggie sticks.
- PASTA TOMATO DRESSING Lot of sun-dried tomato dressing, handful of fresh basil, tsp. oregano, 1 clove garlic, Bragg, lots of fresh tomatoes, olive oil.

Raw Vegetable Juices

Raw vegetable juices are an essential supplement to any diet, particularly in the initial stages of the elimination of accumulated waste and the replenishment of the malnourished organism. All the nutritional elements and nutritional enzymes needed by the cells are found in the juices extracted from fresh raw vegetables, herbs, weeds and fruits. The juices quickly furnish the body with all the necessary vitamins and minerals, minimal energy is utilized and they aid in regulating and normalizing the bowel movement.

Solid food requires many hours of digestion before its nourishment is available to the cells for the body, whereas in the form of juices, nutrients can be digested and assimilated in 10 to 15 minutes after ingestion, with minimum exertion of the digestive system. These juices are then almost totally employed in the nourishment and regeneration of the body's cells, tissues, glands and organs.

Fruit juices are the body cleansers, and they contain all the carboyhydrate and sugar that the body requires. Vegetable juices are the body builders, containing all the amino acids, minerals, salts, enzymes and vitamins required by the body.

One can safely drink as much juice as one can comfortably drink without forcing oneself.

Good juice e.g.s are:

- ½ carrot (or more), ½ spinach.
- ⅓ carrot, ⅓ any greens (kale, watercress, parsley, celery stems and leaves, beet leaves, green sprouts such as sunflower, etc.), ⅓ vegetable of choice e.g. tomato or jicama or other.
- ½ carrot, little beet, the rest celery.
- ¾ carrot (or less), ¼ cabbage.
- ⅓ carrot, ⅓ beet, ⅓ cucumber.

- V8 with a lot of tomatoes combined with any vegetables such as celery, cucumber, parsley, bell pepper, sunflower greens, spinach, arugula. Can add lemon juice and a little Bragg or kelp to taste.

Breakfast Options

1. Milkshakes (see Sweet Section) are an excellent protein-nutrient packed filling breakfast.

2. Citric Fruit or Citric Drinks (not advisable on an empty stomach if you have an extremely acidic blood).

- Sliced citric fruit with or without honey e.g. oranges, pineapple, mandarine, grapefruit, guava, grapes.
- Citric fruit salad combining citric fruits e.g. strawberry, kiwi, guava, pineapple, blueberries, etc. Can top it with whole or coarsely ground sprouted or soaked nuts or seeds.
- Blended or juiced citric drinks e.g. orange and grapefruit or mandarine juice; orange juice blended with pineapple; Orange, pineapple and strawberry; orange juice blended with guava.

3. Melons

- Watermelon, cantaloupe, sweet green melon.

4. Breakfast Cereals

- Sprouted wheat or other grain or nuts and seeds, combined with any sub-acid or sweet fruit (e.g. grated apple or sliced banana), any soaked dried fruit (dates, figs, raisins, prunes), topped with honey, carob, cinnamon or fruit sauce.
- Sprouted wheat or nuts and seeds blended with warm water and strained. Blend the strained milk with any sub-acid or sweet fruit e.g. banana, apple, raisings, mangoes, dates, figs, prunes.

- Sprouted buckwheat or other grain dehydrated. Topped with sliced berries, bananas or other fruits. Serve with milkshake (also referred to as nut milk).

5. Fruit Salad

- Fruit salad composed of fruit of choice topped with: banana, orange juice or water, vanilla, soaked nuts or sprouted seeds. Top with buckwheat sprouted and dehydrated.

Sweet Section

1. Cakes

- Blend in blender or homogenize in food processor: soaked pecans, almonds, yellow raisins, dates (or other soaked nuts and seeds, other soaked dried fruit). Forms base of cake. Top with sliced fruit of choice e.g. mangoes, grapes, strawberries, kiwi.

- Blend or homogenize: soaked nuts, seeds, dried fruit such as raisins and dates. Mix with carrot pulp, carob, cinnamon, honey. Shape and decorate as you desire. Refrigerate.

- Blend: orange juice and soaked cashew nuts, almonds or pecans (or a combination of nuts). Mix with assortment of slice and diced fruit e.g. grated apple, sliced banana, kiwi, strawberry, mango, etc. You can slice the fruit in the food processor. Top with cinnamon and any pretty fruit.

- Homogenize in food processor: 4 mangoes, 7 dates. Add 1 cup soaked and peeled (optional) almonds. Homogenize. Empty into cake container as cake base. Blend: 2 tbs. carob, 1 tbs. honey, 2 mangoes, little vanilla. Pour on top of base. Decorate.

- Thi'ara's Carrot Cake. Blend: 2 cups pitted soaked dates, 2 cups tender coconut flesh, ¼ cup ginger (or less), enough carrot juice to blend. Add: 2 cups carrot pulp, 2 cups chopped walnuts, ½ cup soaked raisins, cinnamon. Crust base: blend soaked almonds and dates or prunes. Icing: blend ¼ kg cashews, orange juice, a little honey.

- Thi'ara's Apple Strudel. Blend or homogenize for cake base: 1/3 kg soaked walnuts (or pecans) and soaked pitted dates. Mix in a bowl: 4 finely chopped apples, 2 grated orange peels, 1 lime, vanilla, cinnamon, 1/3 cup raisins, 1/3 cup kor more pecans or walnuts, 1 cup dates. This is the strudel filling.

- Base: soaked flaxseeds and a little water, blended. Top with a layer of tahini and honey. Top with any fresh or soaked dried fruit or fruit purées e.g. apple purée and strawberry slices.
- Blend: soaked amarynth and oats. Mix with tahini and honey. Sprinkle with sesame seeds. Can make into a cake or small cookies. Refrigerate.
- Soak: peaches in honey and orange juice. Base: soaked and homogenized almonds and dates. Top with a layer of soaked peaches and a layer of crushed soaked pecans and almonds.
- Chocolate pudding. Blend: 4 avocadoes, 2 tbs. carob powder, 3 tbs. honey, 1 tsp. vanilla. Refrigerate.

2. Sweets

An endless variety of candies and cookies can be created from ground or chopped dates, raisins, figs, nuts and seeds. Combine any soaked dried fruits with fresh fruits and nuts or seeds. Add powdered carob if desired. E.g. tahini and honey balls rolled in sesame seed. Refrigerate.

3. Cookies

Delicious cookies are created by blending sunflower seeds or other nuts and seeds (or grains) and fruit or fruit purées. Mix in to batter larger pieces of fruit and nuts. Use vanilla, honey, carob, cinnamon. Dehydrate.

- Blend: sprouted sunflower seeds, coconut, pineapple, strawberries, a little honey.
- Blend: sprouted sunflower seeds, mango, banana, cinnamon.
- Blend: sprouted sunflower and sesame seeds, pecans, banana, carob, honey.
- Ginger Biscuits. Combine: carrot pulp, vanilla, cinnamon, yellow raisins, ginger, dates, some crushed almonds. Variation: use soaked figs.

4. Ice-Creams

All ice-cream is made from cut and peeled frozen fruit such as bananas, strawberries, cantaloupes or any other fruit. Once sufficiently frozen (not too hard), blend or homogenize with a little water or fruit juice or soft fruit if necessary.

Mix different fruits for a variety of flavors. Dates, raisins, cinnamon, carob or honey can be added. Nuts and seeds can also be added. E.g.s banana and strawberry; banana and mango; kiwi, strawberry, mango; frozen mangoes and orange juice.

- Chocolate Ice-Cream. Blend: 5 or 6 large avocados, 3 tbs. honey, 4 tbs. carob powder, vanilla. Set aside. Then blend bananas with vanilla. In a round tupper pour a layer of the avocado-carob mix, then another layer of the banana-vanilla mix. Keep layering until the tupper is full. Freeze. When frozen, flip the tupper upside down on a plate and garnish with strawberries and frozen bananas slices.

5. Milkshakes

All milkshakes are made from sprouted or soaked nuts and seeds. Blend the nuts and seeds in water. Strain. Add and blend the fruit of your choice (fresh, frozen, dried fruit), cinnamon, honey, carob. For a thicker, creamier milkshake, blend with some frozen fruit.

- Blend: almonds, pecans, water. Strain. Blend mango, strawberry, banana, pineapple etc. or a combination of different fruits.
- Chocolate milkshake. Blend: almonds (or other nuts or seeds), banana, 2–3 dates, carob.

Daily Menu

Upon arising:	2–5 lemons in a glass (or less) of water. (Avoid if the blood is so acidic that it causes a negative reaction such as pain).
Breakfast:	Refer to Breakfast Options.
Throughout the Morning:	Any Fruit.
Mid-Morning:	1–2 Vegetable Juices.
Lunch:	Salad and Dressing, Soup or Entrée. (Refer to Chakras 2–6 Recipes).
Mid-Afternoon:	1–2 Vegetable Juices.
Dinner: (6-7 pm)	As for lunch or fruit.
Night:	Fruit

Chakra 2
Recipe Examples

Chakra 2

Chakra 2 consists of: eggs, dairy products, legumes, mushrooms, eggplant, onion, chile and radish. Eggs and dairy products must be eliminated as soon as possible. Goat milk and cheese are good options whilst in transition, as they are not as mucus-forming. Avoid all yellow cheeses. Natural buttermilk, yoghurt, cottage cheese, panela and riqueson are preferable to milk and yellow cheeses.

As the consumption of dairy products results in mucosity and blood acidity, whilst transitioning, one must eat as much fresh fruit and vegetables as possible to counteract these negative side effects.

Do not eat bread (carbohydrate) with cheese (protein), but tortillas and cheese are acceptable. Beans are difficult to digest and also result in blood acidity if eaten in excess. Lentils are the easiest of the legumes to digest. Eat them in cooked soups (Chakra 2) or sprouted (Chakra 5).

Mushrooms and eggplant are excellent healthy non-mucus forming Chakra 2 food options. They are the best meat substitutes owing to their low vibration (just one chakra above meat). They can be sautéed with onion, garlic, herbs, Bragg or soy sauce, and served on tostadas or in tortillas as tacos, with salad and steamed vegetables.

To sautée: place the vegetables in a teflon pan containing olive oil and Bragg or soy sauce. The flame must be extremely low. The oil must never overheat and sizzle. Vegetables are sautéed for 2–5 mins. It is best to first chop the vegetables, steam them, then lightly sautée them for a few minutes, switch off the stove, cover the pan and allow them to continue to cook without the flame.

Although eggplant and mushrooms are proteins, they are not heavy proteins such as the legumes or dairy products. Thus they could mix with grains, depending on your digestion. Try mixing them with different steamed and raw vegetables and / or grains. The fewer food items, the easier it is to digest. Experiment and test your digestive system.

Recipes which contain eggs and dairy products have not been included, as they are not considered healthy food items. However if you are still eating dairy products, all steamed vegetables are good topped with melted cheese. A healthier option is to top the vegetables with creamy nut and seed dressings or any other.

Chakra 2 Recipe Examples

- For any of the legume soups such as lentil soup, split pea soup or sopa de haba in Mexico: cook the legumes in a pot of water for 1 hour. Blend: 8 or more tomatoes, onion, Bragg, parsley or other herbs. Sauté: onion, garlic, diced tomatoes, chopped celery. Mix everything together in the pot. Add salt substitute to taste. For a creamier soup, once cooked, everything can be blended and strained.

- Sauté: mushrooms for 5 mins. with garlic, onion, parsley, Bragg, olive oil. Eat in tacos, on tostadas, or mix with other vegetables and / or grains.

- Eggplant. Peel the eggplant, cut in circles and steam. Blend: tomatoes, garlic, soy sauce, olive oil. Place everything in a pan on a low flame and allow the eggplant to absorb the tomato sauce.

- Eggplant Mushroom Sauté. Steam: eggplant, mushrooms, onion, red or yellow bell pepper. Sauté for a few mins. with quick-blended tomatoes, Bragg, olive oil, a pinch of rosemary or Italian herbs. Turn off stove and cover. Let sit for 5 mins.

- Steam mushrooms. Allow them to simmer in sauce of your choice e.g. Mexican Salsa Verde (under Chili Dressing Examples) or other.

Chakra 3
Recipe Examples

Chakra 3

Chakra 3 consists of: the Complex Carbohydrates (grains, pastas, bread, tortillas, potatoes and other tubercles, corn on the cob), Seaweed, Avocado and Tofu.

In a Chakra 2 diet, one should eat approximately 60% raw and 40% Chakra 2 or above food. In a Chakra 3 diet, eat about 70% raw and 30% Chakra 3 or above cooked. Bear in mind that the cooked carbohydrates also create blood acidity and high levels of mucosity, if consumed in excess over the years. The organic minerals in carbohydrates become inorganic once cooked and cannot be assimilated. Eat Chakra 3 in small amounts.

Chakra 3 Recipe Examples

1. Potatoes

- Baked or Steamed. Serve with olive oil, salt substitute and seasoning.
- French Fries. Cut potato for French fries. Steam until cooked. Place in oven 30–40 mins. until golden. Serve with olive oil, sea salt or other substitute and seasonings.
- Mashed Potato. Steam potatoes using clean water. When cooked, mash them with the steaming water and some olive oil, sea salt or Bragg. Can be mixed with diced, steamed carrot, peas, or any other vegetable. Mash sweet potato too.
- Stuffed Potato. Cut potatoes in half and steam. Once cooked hollow out some potato and mix it with diced steam & / raw vegetables e.g. carrots, mushrooms, zucchini, red and green pepper. Stuff potatoes attractively with the purée mix.
- Sliced Potato Circles. Use white or sweet potato. Steam. Place in oven. Serve with seasonings.
- Potato and Tomato mix. Dice potatoes and steam cook. Sauté for 2–5 mins. in Bragg or soy sauce, a little olive oil, onion, garlic (optional), parsley or other herbs. Add diced tomatoes. Add cooked potatoes.
- Potatoes and Bragg. Steam the cut potatoes. Sauté with Bragg, olive oil, onion, green pepper (or other vegetable).

- Chili Potatoes. Steam diced potatoes and chili of choice finely cut. Sauté with Bragg, onion, garlic (optional).
- Potato Patti. Make mashed potato. Form patties and cook until golden on heated teflon pan, without oil. Serve with olive oil and sea salt.

2. Tostadas or Tacos

Tostadas are made with tortillas on an Earthenware or metal dish or in a teflon pan on a low flame, no oil. Good tostada toppings are: finely shredded lettuce, onion, radish.

The following can be put on tostadas or eaten in tortillas as tacos:

- Raw tomato and onion with olive oil and sea salt or Bragg.
- Avocado, tomato, onion, cilantro, parsley, basil or other herb, fresh green or red chili (optional), Bragg, olive oil (optional), top with alfalfa sprouts.
- Potato and Tomato mix (see Potatoes).
- Sautéed Mushrooms. Sauté 5 mins. with garlic, parsley, Bragg, olive oil.
- Mashed Potato with avocado dressing, shredded lettuce and sliced radish on top.
- Salad Tacos with dressing of choice.

3. Carbohydrate and Vegetable Mixes

- Cooked potatoes, rice or other grain, pasta. Mix with raw & / cooked steamed or sautéed diced or shredded vegetables, olive oil, Bragg, seasonings. E.g. rice, corn, peas, carrots. Steam then dice veggies of choice: shredded cabbage, diced chayote, zucchini, peas, green or red bell peppers, broccoli and cauliflower florets. Add to pasta, with olive oil and salt substitute, seasoning, lemon (optional). Can make red Mexican rice by cooking rice in blended tomato sauce.
- Spaghetti and Tomato Sauce. Tomato Sauce (can be used to top steamed veggies or in tacos): Sauté the following 5 mins. in Bragg and olive oil—chopped onion, garlic, green pepper, celery. Add diced tomatoes, basil, Italian herbs. Blend: tomatoes, onion, Bragg. Mix all together.

4. Taboule

- Soak bulgur wheat 1–3 hours, until soft. Chop tomato, onion or chives, parsley, mint. Mix everything with olive oil, lemon and Bragg. Serve on large lettuce leaves. Eat with home-made tostadas or corn tortillas.

5. Pozole

- Cook 1–2 cups wheat. Place 8–12 whole tomatoes in teflon pan, no oil, allow to cook 5 mins. Boil 6–12 chili guajillos (deveined, no seeds). Blend chilis and tomatoes with Bragg, onion, garlic, olive oil. Mix all together with cooked corn kernels and mushrooms.

6. Tofu Dishes

Tofu is a protein and should not be combined with carbohydrates such as rice, potato or pasta. It combines well with corn tortilla however. Eat it with steamed or sautéed vegetable mixes, or better still, with salad. Sauté tofu with any steamed vegetables such as mushrooms, bell peppers, onions, tomatoes, etc. Serve with different sauces.

- Simple tofu. Sauté sliced tofu in Teflon pan with Bragg, no oil, until golden. Can add curry powder, tumeric, cayenne or any other herb or spice.
- Tofu Cheese. Cut or mash tofu. Eat unseasoned or with lemon, Bragg, or other seasoning. Can be added to salads or steamed veggie mixes.
- Miso Soup. Heat water until hot but not boiling. Add seaweed such as hijiki or nori, chopped chives, miso and chunks of tofu. Stir, let sit a few mins. and serve.

Chakra 4
Recipe Examples

Chakra 4

Chakra 4 consists of: Lightly steamed or sautéed vegetables, lightly cooked vegetable soups, all dehydrated foods, nuts and seeds, cooked nopales (raw they are difficult to digest).

Chakra 4 is closer to the elimination pole (Chakra 6), than to the accumulation pole (Chakra 1). A Chakra 4 and above diet is appropriate for this era, enabling us to eliminate all accumulated excesses owing to incorrect dietary habits over the years.

Chakra 4 lightly cooked vegetables do not create mucosity or acidity. They are a great transition to raw food.

Chakra 4 Recipe Example

1. Steamed and Sautéed Vegetable Dishes

Steam any vegetables whole, diced, sliced or grated. Cut vegetables must cook for less time. Leaves such as swiss chard steam for a minute or less; root vegetables such as beet or carrots for 10–15 mins. Most other vegetables for 5 mins. or less.

In a pan sautée onions, garlic and herbs of choice in olive oil and soy sauce (or any sauce of choice). The flame must be extremely low and one cooks for no more than 2 mins. with the flame, then turn off the stove but cover the pan with a lid. The oil must never sizzle.

Mix the steamed vegetables with the onion and garlic etc. Experiment with a variety of attractive vegetable cuts. Sprinkle with kelp, cayenne, garlic and onion powder, or dried herbs.

Not all the vegetables can be steamed together. First steam the ones that take longer, remove them from the steamer, and continue with ones that take but a few minutes.

Good vegetables to steam are: carrots, broccoli, cauliflower, cabbage, beets, zucchini, green beans, onions, asparagus, chayote, corn, mushrooms, eggplant, snow peas, brussel sprouts.

Examples:

- Steamed carrots, broccoli, asparagus, peas—mixed with sautéed onion.
- Steamed green beans, chayote, cauliflower—mixed with sautéed onion.
- Shredded cabbage, mung sprouts, celery, red and green pepper, carrot, broccoli—mixed with sautéed onion and mushroom.
- Artichokes (steam for approx. 40 mins.) with basil or other dressing.
- Nopales—placed in hot water for approx. 30 mins. Cut in strips and serve with cilantro, diced onion and tomato. Add lemon, olive oil, sea salt or soy sauce.
- Alternative—small nopales placed in pan with soy sauce and a little water. Cook on very low flame for 10 mins.
- Eggplant—peel and slice thinly. Steam. Blend: tomatoes, garlic, soy sauce. Cook everything in pan for 10 to 15 mins, allowing the eggplant to absorb the sauce.
- Green leaves such as purslane, swiss or chinese chard, tatsoy—steam for less than 1 min. Serve with lemon, sea salt, kelp, soy sauce, olive oil.
- Chop Suey—sautée onion, green bell pepper and mushrooms in olive oil and soy sauce for 1–2 mins. Cover it. Add the following vegetables cut in thin strips and steamed: broccoli, jicama, carrot, zucchini, mung sprouts.
- Stir Fry. Dehydrated and diced or sliced: onion or chives, mushrooms, broccoli florets, zucchini (long thin strips), celery, red and green or yellow bell pepper, eggplant. Raw, diced or long thin strips: carrots, jicama, mung sprouts, peas, beet, almonds (small pieces). Combine. Dressing: Bragg, oil, orange juice.

2. Vegetable Soups

- Cream of any vegetable such as broccoli, mushroom, chayote, carrot, etc. Steam the vegetable(s) using clean water. When cooked, blend the vegetables with the water used for steaming. Sauté garlic, onion, celery, parsley or any other vegetable or herb in olive oil and soy sauce.

Mix everything together. Part of the steamed vegetables or herbs can be blended, and part chopped up and mixed in afterwards. Soups can be blended with any soaked nuts or seeds such as pecans, almonds, sunflower seeds. Top soups with: cubed avocado, chopped parsley, oregano, basil, chives, arugula, cilantro, diced tomato, radish, onion, celery.

- Blend vegetables such as tomato, avocado (optional for thicker, creamier soup), onion, garlic, Bragg. Cut vegetables (grate in food processor if you have one) such as zucchini, carrots, celery, cauliflower, green leaves, peas. Heat water and mix blended and cut vegetables together to make a soup.

- Boil a pot of water and add any cut vegetables of choice, kelp, soy sauce, chile (optional). Cover and allow to sit for 15 mins. Can add sautéed onion, garlic, herbs. Alternatively can blend tomatoes, onion, garlic, any other vegetables, herbs, and add it.

3. Dehydrated Vegetables

All dehydrated food corresponds to Chakra 4. The more dehydrated i.e. the more concentrated (the less water), the more difficult it is to digest and the lower the vibration. All dehydrated food is dehydrated in a dehydrator at 100–105° F, no higher. Alternatively it is sun baked and enriched with the sun's potent energy.

Quick and easy vegetables to dehydrate are: eggplant, tomatoes, onion, red and green pepper, mushrooms, shredded cabbage, small broccoli and cauliflower florets, zucchini, beetroot, spinach or other leaves. Slice vegetables as desired. The thinner the slices the faster the dehydrating time. Vegetables can be marinated the night before in olive oil and soy sauce or any other sauce e.g. add chile, herbs. Herbs and spices can also be added once marinated, just before dehydrating. If you haven't marinated your vegetables and you want a quick dehydrated dish, slice veggies, top with oil, soy sauce and herbs of choice. Dehydrate for half an hour to one hour. Eat warm.

4. Dehydrated Bread and Crackers

For breads and crackers you can use any sprouted grains, nuts and seeds, grated or finely chopped vegetables (for salty crackers), or soaked dried fruit or blended fruit (for sweet cookies). The nuts and seed crackers produce less mucosity. I do not recommend eating grain bread too much.

All breads and crackers are blended in the blender or homogenized in the food processor or Green Life machine. The better the food processor, the less liquid is needed to homogenize the nuts, seeds and grains.

- Blend soaked or sprouted sunflower and sesame seeds with miso, Bragg or other salt substitute, onion, garlic (optional), water. Make thin, crisp crackers or thicker moister breads. Try a variety of nut and seed mixtures, yielding different cracker flavors e.g. almonds and pecan with caraway seeds. Add chopped or grated vegetables (fresh and dehydrated) of choice.
- Blend: 3 cups sesame seed, 3 tomatoes, ½ green bell pepper, ¼ garlic clove, ¼ small onion, Bragg.
- Blend: 3 cups sprouted wheat (or other grain such as kamut), little olive oil, ¼ or more cup orange juice. Add blended nuts and seeds, or vegetables or fruit.
- Tomato Bread. Blend grains or nuts and seeds with Bragg, onion and many tomatoes. Can mix in sun-dried tomatoes, grated carrot, red bell pepper, green leaves finely cut, cut mushrooms, or anything else. Herbs such as basil and oregano are good.
- Chile Bread. Blend: 2 cups wheat, 3 dates, 3 tomatoes, little garlic, 3 tbs. olive oil, chili ancho, lot of chile guajillo, water to blend.
- Pumpernickel Bread. Blend: 2 cups wheat, 2 tbs. carob, 2 tsp. caraway seeds, ¼ cup olive oil.
- Flax Crax. Soak and blend: flax seeds, Bragg, onion, water. Form thin crackers.
- Sweet Bread. Blend: ¼ cup almonds, ¼ cup pecans, 2 cups grains, ½ cup grated apple, 3 dates, orange juice, little olive oil. If do not want it sweet, blend with less orange juice, more water, garlic, parsley. If want it like real whole wheat baked bread, use no liquid and homogenize in food processor or Green Life machine.
- Carrot Bread. Blend: any grain, fresh oregano, cayenne, a little garlic, a little onion, tomato, grated carrot, olive oil, Bragg.
- For sweet cookies add soaked dried dates, figs or yellow raisins. Can add mango, banana, apple or other purée. Add honey, vanilla, cinnamon, carob when desired. Grated coconut and honey dehydrated yield delicious cookies.

- Banana (mango, strawberry etc.) Cookies. Blend grains or sunflower seeds, banana, vanilla, cinnamon, date.

5. Nuts and Seeds

All nuts and seeds should be soaked at least 4 hours before using, thus releasing the enzyme inhibitors, facilitating digestion. Best is to soak them during the night. Nuts generally do not sprout, but seeds do. Sprouting raises the vibration as they are more nutritive and easier to digest.

All nuts and seeds are healthiest unsalted and raw. Avoid peanuts and cashews as they are too hard on the digestion. Coconuts are excellent provided they are soft. If hard, they can be blended with their water and strained. Soft coconuts can be blended with their water and left unstrained if desired. The coconut water is highly nutritious.

- Nut and seed drinks. Blend a handful of soaked or sprouted nuts and seeds with plenty water e.g. almonds and pecans or almonds and sesame seeds, etc. Strain. Blend strained nut-seed milk with any fruit of your choice e.g. mangoes, strawberries, banana. Can add honey, vanilla, cinnamon, carob. This is a highly nutritious easily digested protein shake.

Chakra 5
Recipe Examples

Chakra 5

Chakra 5 consists of: raw vegetable soups and salads, vegetable drinks, sprouts, green leaves and weeds.

This is a purely raw food diet, and the healthiest, once the body and mind are ready for it.

Chakra 5 Recipe Examples

1. Entrées

- Guacamole. Dice: tomatoes, onion, cilantro (cucumber, bell peppers, celery, green leaves, or anything else of your choice). Mash avocadoes and add olive oil, lemon, Bragg. Combine.
- Ceviche. Dice and combine: mushrooms, tomatoes, onion, cilantro, fresh red or green chili (optional), pieces of nori (optional). Dressing: Bragg, lemon, olive oil. Variation: add radish & / red and green bell peppers.
- Taboule. Dice and combine: tomatoes, onion or chives, green & / red bell pepper, cucumber, watercress, parsley, mint (or cilantro), olives (optional). Add sprouted wheat slightly blended for easier digestion. Dressing: Bragg, lemon, olive oil.
- Garbanzo Dip. Homogenize in food processor: sprouted garbanzos (or any sprouted nuts and seeds), olive oil, Bragg, lemon, parsley & / cilantro, garlic (optional). Add water for a creamier dressing, no water or very little for a thicker dip. Variation: add fresh chili for a spicy dip. Variation: add finely diced vegetables and herbs to the dip e.g.diced onions, chives, carrots, celery, radish, bell peppers, cilantro, parsley. Variation: try adding other vegetables such as carrots, red peppers, chives, etc. when homogenizing in the food processor. Variation: add sesame seeds to the dip. The dip can be used to stuff bell peppers or tomatoes or as a dip for vegetable sticks such as carrots, celery, jicama, cucumber. Note: garbanzos must be soaked for two nights in order for them to sprout. The water must be changed daily. They are extremely hard on the digestive system. Avoid them if your digestion is weak.

- Hamburger Patties. Blend and dehydrate or sun dry in the form of patties: Sprouted lentils, sprouted wheat or other grain, soaked or sprouted nuts and seeds with Bragg, onion, water, garlic (optional). Add any chopped or grated vegetables to the batter e.g. onions, carrots, celery, mushrooms, beet, red bell peppers, radish. Do not blend green bell peppers, cilantro or large quantities of greens and herbs as they create bitter patties. Mix in chopped herbs or greens by hand after the initial blending. Patties can be thoroughly dried or left slightly moist (the moister the easier to digest). They can be sprinkled with sesame or sunflower seed, or almond meal. Serve with catsup (see Simple Salad Dressings, Sun-Dried Tomato Dressing Examples). Hamburger Patti e.g. Blend: 1 cup nuts, 1 cup almonds, 1 cup mushrooms, 2/3 cup water or vegetable juice, Bragg. Mix in: ½ cup grated carrots, ¼ cup onion. Form patties and dehydrate.

- Gazpacho. Blend any of the following with or without water, depending on the desired consistency. If you wish to blend without water, start by blending the tomatoes first, then add the rest. Blend: many ripe tomatoes, cucumber, celery, red bell pepper, onion, little parsley, cilantro, basil or any other herb. Can add lemon, olive oil, Bragg. Combines well with crackers topped with avocado, tomato and alfalfa sprouts.

- Seed Cheeses. Blend equal amounts of sprouted sunflower seeds, sesame seeds and water. Allow the mixture to ferment by leaving out of the refrigerator for approx. 8 hours. Can strain the mixture for a more condensed seed cheese. Variation: add finely chopped vegetables before or after fermentation e.g. radish, bell peppers, olives, celery, parsley, cilantro, arugula. Add kelp or other seaweed, Bragg or miso.

- Nut and Seed Loaves. These are made in the same way as the seed cheeses. The nuts and seeds must be soaked overnight. The nut-seed mix can be fermented or unfermented. A wide variety of diced herbs and vegetables can be added to the seed loaves before or after fermentation. Good vegetables are: bell peppers, celery, mushrooms, onions, carrots, beetroot, radishes. Desirable herbs are: oregano, basil, parsley, cilantro, marjoram, rosemary, thyme. The loaf can be placed in the sun or dehydrator for several hours if desired. A recipe example:—Blend with as little water as possible: 1 ½ cups walnuts, sunflower seeds and almonds (4 ½ cups in all). Stir in: 1 tbs. minced garlic, 1 tbs. chopped onion, ½ tbs. sea salt, ½ cup chopped parsley, ½

41

cup chopped celery, some minced ginger (optional), any herb of choice, 1 cup chopped red bell pepper, 1 tbs. (or less) fresh chili, olive oil, cumin seeds.

- Stuffed Vegetables. Vegetables such as bell peppers, large tomatoes and avocados can be stuffed with: garbanzo or nut-seed dips (does not combine with avocado) with or without diced vegetables; guacamole; vegetable loaves; taboule; ceviche; sprouts or grated vegetables and dressings.

- Tacos. Tacos can be created with large lettuce, chard or other green leaves, or with nori sheets. A variety of fillings can be created: seed cheeses or loaves; vegetable sticks or grated veggies and a dressing. E.g. nori sheets filled with seed cheese or fermented vegetables and lots of alfalfa sprouts. Or nori sheets or lettuce leaves filled with carrot, cucumber and celery sticks, alfalfa sprouts and avocado dressing.

- Quiche. Blend: 2 cups corn, 1/8 cup flax seed pulverized in blender (dry), 1/3 cup chopped cilantro, little ginger (optional), 1 small onion, ½ cup orange juice, few tbs. olive oil, 1 chili chipotle or habanero or cayenne, ½ cup sun-dried tomatoes. Stir in any sliced or finely chopped vegetables such as mushrooms, spinach, bell peppers, tomatoes. Place in pie pan, no more than 2 inches thick, and decorate with sliced fresh tomatoes, bell peppers, mushrooms. Dehydrate overnight.

- Nopales. Soak small tender nopales in warm water for an hour or more, until soft. Dice: nopales, tomatoes, onion, cilantro, radishes (optional). Add: olive oil, Bragg or sea salt.

- Hot Mexican Nopales. Soak nopales until soft. Blend: chili ancho, guajillo, garlic, onion, clove, oregano. Cut nopales and mix with sauce and diced cilantro.

- Chili Rellenos. Peel chili poblanos with a vegetable peeler and soak in hot water for min. 1 hr. Blend: soaked pecans and almonds, Bragg, onion, garlic, cilantro, a few tomatoes, oil (optional). Add to blended sauce: sliced mushrooms, chopped radish, chives, bell peppers, cilantro or parsley, chili serrano or jalapeno. Fill chili poblanos with sauce and top with sprouts.

- Fermented cabbage or other vegetables. (Fermented foods are enzyme packed, very nutritious and easy to digest). Homogenize cabbage in food processor with the "S" blade. Can add kelp. Place in glass jar and allow to ferment for a few days at room temperature. Experiment with other vegetables and vegetable combinations. The longer it ferments, the tangier the taste.

- Tuna. Serves 6. Blend: ½ kg pecans, ½ kg sunflower seeds, little ginger, Bragg, juice of 3 lemons. Chop and mix in: 2 small onions, 4 celery stalks, 1½ red bell peppers, 1½ cups parsley.

- Fried Rice. Sprouted wild rice, kamut or quinoa or best, but wheat could be used too. Mix with chopped vegetables such as bell peppers, diced tomatoes, onion, mushrooms, celery, etc. Eat with oil, Bragg, lemon and herbs of choice.

2. Salads

The best way to make a good salad is to always have a supply of sprouts sprouting, and to keep a variety of fresh vegetables and greens in your refrigerator, or ideally, in your garden. When you are about to eat, feel which vegetables you feel like, and feel whether you feel like a heavier seed or avocado dressing, or a lighter one.

I do not advise keeping leftover salads. They are never as appetizing or nutritious. Leftovers can be used for salad dressings which can be stored for a few days in the refrigerator, or for blended drinks or soups which can be refrigerated and used the same day.

The heavier dressings especially enliven hard, crunchy vegetable salads composed of e.g. carrots, celery, shredded cabbage, radish, beet, jicama.
Or they can be used as dips.

I am providing very few salad examples, as salad recipes are redundant. It is more tedious to follow someone else's recipe, than to simply create your own. Aim at diversity. Be creative. Vary the dressings, cuts, and vegetables used in the salads. Experiment. Visual appeal is extremely important—select attractive plates, bowls and cutlery, and take the extra five minutes to arrange the food artistically, even if it is only for yourself, so that the food is appetizing. Raw food is so colorful, so beautiful. Flowers add an exquisite touch.

- Variety Salad. Use any or all of the following green leaves: watercress, different organic lettuces, kale, arugula, Chinese or Swiss chard, spinach, purslane, lambsquarters, etc. Different herbs like basil, cilantro, parsley, oregano, mint. Any weeds such as lambsquarters, purslane, dandelion, etc. Utilize any raw vegetables, being creative with different cuts: tomato, red, green or yellow bell pepper, cucumber, carrot, jicama, onion, celery, radish, mushrooms, zucchini, chayote, cabbage. Make use of easy to grow, fresh sprouts such as mung, lentils, alfalfa, radish, fenugreek, trebol. Vary your dressings (see Salad Dressing chapter).

- Coleslaw Variations. Combine any of the following: cabbage, carrot, beet, radish, jicama, celery, any of the bell peppers.

- Creamy Curried Carrot Salad. Combine: 5 cups grated carrots, 1 cup soaked yellow raisins, 1 ½ cups celery finely chopped, 1/3 cup minced parsley, ½ cup finely chopped pecans. Dressing. Blend till creamy: 2 cups soaked pecans, juice of 2–3 oranges, ¼ cup olive oil (or less and add water), pinch of cumin, pinch of cayenne, ½ tsp. curry, 1 tbs. Bragg. Mix salad and dressing.

- Salad: Shredded spinach leaves topped with diced cucumber and tomato. Dressing: Light Sesame Seed Dressing.

- Salad: Sliced tomatoes, cucumber and onion rings. Dressing: Mustard Vinagrette.

- Salad: Mushrooms, onions, tomatoes, bell peppers, cucumbers, jicama. Dressing: Vegetable Carrot Dressing.

- Salad: Large cubed tomato, jicama, bell peppers, celery. Add finely chopped chili serrano. Dressing: any Nut-Seed Dressing or Garbanzo Dressing.

- Salad: Fairly finely diced tomatoes, radish, cucumber, bell peppers. Dressing: Lemon, kelp (sea salt or Bragg), cayenne.

- Finger Salad: Sticks of jicama, cucumber, carrot, celery, cauliflower and broccoli florets (if too difficult to digest, steam lightly), etc. Dressing: any of the Chili Dressings, Avocado Dressings, or Nut-Seed Dressings.

- Salad: Diced: tomatoes, onions, radishes. Finely chopped: kale, spinach, cilantro, parsley, watercress. Combine. Salad Dressing: Tomatoes, chili serrano, Bragg, olive oil.

- Stir Fry: shredded cabbage, chopped broccoli, carrots—julienne, long thin celery sticks, finely sliced red and green bell peppers, mushroom finely sliced, small pieces of finely sliced ginger. Dressing: olive oil, Bragg, vinegar, orange juice.

- Greens and Weed Salad: mixture of any greens, weeds & / sprouts. Serve with Nut-Seed Dressing or Light Sesame Dressing.
- Lentil Sprout Salad: lentil sprouts, celery, cilantro, tomato, green pepper, onion. Dressing: Bragg or seaweed and lemon.

As you can see, salad recipes are unnecessary. Good dressings and sauces make any salad tasty. Experiment with all the dressings in the Simple Salad Dressing chapter, and then using those dressings as a base, create your own dressings and salads.

3. Soups

Soups can be eaten at room temperature, warmed in the sun, or heated on an extremely low flame for no more than a few minutes. Alternatively place the soup in a pyrex dish and then in a large bowl of hot water.

A variety of delicious soups can be easily and simply created using blended and juiced vegetables as the broth, and combined with chopped vegetables.

These examples are provided to give you an idea of some vegetable soup combinations.

- Blend with a lot of warm water: fresh tomatoes, sun-dried tomatoes, a little beet, red bell pepper, a little celery, a little carrot, chili of choice (jalapeno, serrano, guajillo, cayenne), cebollin, avocado (optional).
- Juice in extractor: many carrots (approx. 15), 1 red pepper, a little parsley. Blend with: ½ red chili serrano, parsley, 5–10 arugula leaves, 3 medium tomatoes, onion greens, ½ avocado, salt substitute.
- Chop and top with: lots of greens such as arugula, chives, purslane, parsley, cilantro, watercress. Add cubed avocado.
- Blend: tomatoes, some avocado, a little chili of choice, chives, cilantro, a little carrot juice, 2–3 stems of celery juice, juice of 1 red bell pepper. Add zucchini flowers (stems removed) which have been soaked in warm water for 15 mins. Top with chopped onion, tomato, cilantro, celery, avocado cubes.
- Lentil Soup. Blend: many tomatoes, 1 red bell pepper, cilantro, chives or onion, 1–2 sticks celery juice, a little carrot juice, red jalapeno,

Bragg. Add: chopped onion, tomato, cilantro, celery (optional). Mix everything with lentil sprouts. Eat with greens such as arugula.

- Makes 1 serving. Blend: ½ avocado, 6–8 medium tomatoes, a little onion, a lot of cilantro, a little chili jalapeno, approx. 1/3 cup celery stem and leaves. Combine with finely chopped greens e.g.: purslane, tap soy, Swiss and Chinese chard, a little mustard greens, celery stem and some leaves, parsley, onion, cilantro, watercress, arugula. Add cubed avocado.

- Gazpacho. Serves 6. Blend: 2 kg tomatoes, 2 red bell peppers, 1 green bell pepper, cilantro, garlic, 3 celery stalks, 2 cucumbers, ½ small onion, 2 lemons, Bragg.

- Split Pea Soup. Blend: 1 cup fresh peas, ½ cup carrot juice, ½ cup celery juice, 1 onion, garlic, 1 avocado, dulse, Bragg. Top with chopped parsley.

- Vegetable Cream Soup. Blend: ½ cup pecans, 1 cup water, 2 cups chopped vegetables e.g. onion, garlic, celery, spinach, broccoli, carrots, mushrooms. Top with parsley or other herbs and sprouts.

- Quick Soup. Blend: 1 cup carrot juice, 1 cup celery juice, 1 cup grated cabbage, 1 red bell pepper, 1 tomato, ½ avocado, a little cayenne, a little Bragg.

- Avocado Soup. Blend: 3 tomatoes, ½ cucumber, 1 stalk celery, ½ onion, 1 tbs. chopped parsley, 2 avocadoes, juice of 3 lemons, Bragg. Top with sprouts.

- Cream of Spinach Soup. Blend: 2 cups tomato, celery and carrot juice, 2 cups spinach, ½ avocado, little garlic, 1 tbs. jalapeno, 1 tbs. ginger, 2 tbs. onion, 1 tbs. mint, 1/3 cup cilantro, Bragg, juice of 1 lemon, little oil.

Chakra 6
Recipe Examples

Chakra 6

The Chakra 6 diet is extremely simple, consisting of fruit, fruit drinks and green chlorophyll drinks. The green chlorophyll drinks consist of green juices mixed with citric juices e.g. comfrey, parsley, chaya, celery juice combined with orange, mandarine, grapefruit, pineapple, kiwi, lemon. Strain. Try combining greens with apple juice.

In Chakra 6 one consumes more liquids than solids.

The closer one approaches Chakra 6, the less garlic is tolerated. Salt substitutes such as Bragg can no longer be used and will produce an adverse reaction such as congestion or a sore throat. Spicy vegetables such as onion, radish, a little chili or cayenne (if it can still be tolerated), can be used, in addition to spicy green leaves such as chives or arugula, to help overcome the salt craving.

One never jumps to a Chakra 6 diet. It is something that occurs naturally and gradually, and you are guided by the energies. Chakra 6 is an energetic experience, the diet reflects the experience. The energies fluctuate, being more Cosmic at times, more Kundalini at other times. The more Cosmic the energy, the more liquids are desired, the best being fruit purées or juices, or green juices mixed with citric juices. The more Kundalini the energy, the more one may want mild vegetable juices or vegetable blended mixtures.

Chakra 6 Recipe Examples

For green drinks, blend any green leaves with any citric fruit or combination of citric fruits. Examples of green leaves or green vegetables are: parsley, spinach, alfalfa, chaya, comfrey, sorrel, malva, celery, cucumber. Examples of citric fruits are: orange, grapefruit, mandarine, pineapple, guava, strawberry, grape, lemon.

Make half a liter of citric juice and add it to half a liter of greens and water, blended and strained.

Juice examples are:

- Orange (or mandarine or grapefruit) and parsley, spinach, comfrey or chaya.

- 4-6 oranges (or honey), 3 lemons, 6–8 leaves of comfrey (or other green), water.
- 6 oranges, 1 lemon (or more), 1 cucumber, 1 stalk of celery (or more), a little parsley, any other green leaves, a little water.
- Apple juice with celery and ginger.
- Alfalfa, lemon, honey, water.
- Alfalfa, orange, pineapple, water.
- Spinach, 3 lemons, pineapple, orange, water.
- Orange, lemon, chaya, guava.

The Power of the Mind

Nutrition and close contact with the natural elements is a fundamental factor contributing to health. Daily one should aspire to eating protein and healthy fats such as avocado or nuts and seeds, fruit, greens, and some seaweed. Variety is a key element. The vegetable juices and green leaves can furnish the body with all the minerals it requires.

With diet, as with everything, balance and moderation are required. You cannot go to either extreme for too long. For example if you are on a Chakra 5 and 6 diet for a long time and experiencing high Cosmic Energy, after some time, you may need to drop to a Chakra 4 diet to balance yourself. The Chakra 5 and 6 foods are highly Yin and expansive. You will need to balance this after time with the more Yang, concentrated food of Chakra 4, in order to avoid too much expansion which could result in water retention, feeling out of harmony, experiencing energetic imbalances.

Watch your moods. If you are feeling unbalanced, check that your diet is neither too high nor too low (vibration), too strict nor too slack, etc. Balance it.

Adequate rest is basic to health too. Rest signifies not living a stressful life. Living and working the chakra experience that corresponds to your evolution. Contact with the earth, fresh air, sun exposure, clean water, are all important. An integral exercise such as Yoga, which works the physical, emotional and mental bodies, and enables the connection with the Spirit, must be practiced daily. This daily spiritual nourishment is too often overlooked by health practitioners.

We have to constantly be reminded of the enormous power of the mind. Thoughts are energy and energy creates and affects everything. Thoughts are things, which manifest physically. Every thought has a shape, form and color.

The subconscious mind does not differentiate between a thought and an actual event. The body reacts to a negative (or positive) thought as though it was actually experiencing the event.

50

Everything that we think, is manifested externally in our bodies and in our lives. We are responsible for our own life and death and no virus or circumstance can bring illness upon us.

Anxiety and stressful thinking and living weaken the whole body, regardless of how pure and nourishing the diet.

Strong, pure, creative, happy thoughts build a strong, pure, balanced body. The body is a highly sensitive, finely tined instrument, which responds to all thoughts all the time. Thought patterns—positive or negative—are producing positive or negative effects on the body constantly.

The body can be restructured and rejuvenated by changing one's diet and restructuring one's thought patterns. A different body plan has to be sent to the subconscious mind.

We are creators of our lives, not victims. Coincidence, good or bad luck does not exist. Perfect order and justice exist in the Universe. There is a just reason for everything.

Hatha Yoga, Pranayama and Meditation are great, powerful tools which enable one to purify and restructure oné mind. To master life one has to master one's mind. Mind mastery requires focusing only on positive, elevating divine thoughts.

Joy, freedom, love, knowledge, real bliss are our birthrights. We have to learn how to stop limiting ourselves, how to beware of the thoughts we are harboring; how to regain our force.

Yoga and correct Nutrition are two potent tools, which purify and strengthen the body, emotions, mind and Spirit.

Our destiny lies within our thoughts.

0-595-28425-6

Printed in the United States
108157LV00004B/23/A